TEAM SPIRIT®

SMART BOOKS FOR YOUNG FANS

THE BALTIMORE RAVENS

BY
MARK STEWART

NORWOOD HOUSE PRESS

CHICAGO, ILLINOIS

Norwood House Press
P.O. Box 316598
Chicago, Illinois 60631

For information regarding Norwood House Press, please visit our website at:
www.norwoodhousepress.com or call 866-565-2900.

All photos courtesy of Getty Images except the following:
Topps, Inc. (10, 15, 21, 35 top left & right, 40, 41, 42 top & bottom left), SportsChrome (11, 31),
Sports Illustrated/TIME Inc. (23), Black Book Partners (28, 43 right), Author's Collection (33),
The Upper Deck Company (34), The Sporting News (43 left), Matt Richman (48).
Cover Photo: Icon SMI

The memorabilia and artifacts pictured in this book are presented for educational and informational purposes,
and come from the collection of the author.

Editor: Mike Kennedy
Designer: Ron Jaffe
Project Management: Black Book Partners, LLC.
Special thanks to Topps, Inc.

Library of Congress Cataloging-in-Publication Data

Stewart, Mark, 1960-
   The Baltimore Ravens / by Mark Stewart. -- Rev. ed.
      p. cm. -- (Team spirit)
   Includes bibliographical references and index.
   Summary: "A revised Team Spirit Football edition featuring the Baltimore
Ravens that chronicles the history and accomplishments of the team. Includes
access to the Team Spirit website which provides additional information and
photos"--Provided by publisher.
   ISBN 978-1-59953-514-2 (library edition : alk. paper) -- ISBN
978-1-60357-456-3 (ebook)
   1. Baltimore Ravens (Football team)--History--Juvenile literature. I.
Title.
   GV956.B3S84 2012
   796.332'64097526--dc23

                                              2012016232

Manufactured in the United States of America in North Mankato, Minnesota.
205N—082012

COVER PHOTO: The Ravens stand tall after making a key stop on defense.

Table of Contents

ABOUT OUR GLOSSARY

In this book, there may be several words that you are reading for the first time. Some are sports words, some are new vocabulary words, and some are familiar words that are used in an unusual way. All of these words are defined on page 46. Throughout the book, sports words appear in **bold type**. Regular vocabulary words appear in ***bold italic type***.

Meet the Ravens

Each season when the **National Football League (NFL)** announces its schedule, the first thing many players do is check to see if their team is going to play the Baltimore Ravens. It is guaranteed that this will be the least enjoyable game of the year. The Ravens are known for their size, speed, and intelligence. They are also known for their physical play.

No team in football relies more on its defense to win games. The Ravens specialize in making life difficult for opposing offenses. The Baltimore defense doesn't just shut down teams—it can put points on the scoreboard, too.

This book tells the story of the Ravens. They are one of football's newest teams, but they win games the old-fashioned way—with hard tackling and powerful blocking. That is the Baltimore way. The Ravens don't know any other way to play.

Ed Reed and Ray Lewis get fired up after a good play. The Ravens are known for their excellent defense.

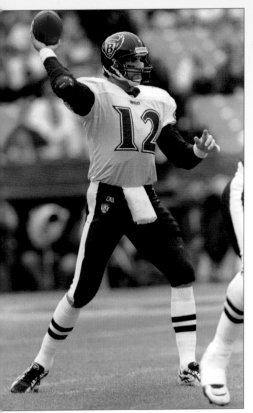

ans in Baltimore, Maryland, will never forget the day in 1984 that their beloved Colts left town for Indianapolis, Indiana. They adored their team. They begged the NFL to give them a new team. For more than 10 years, the people of Baltimore waited. Finally, in 1996, the NFL announced that Art Modell—the owner of the Cleveland Browns—would move his team to Baltimore. The new team would be called the Ravens, and they would play in the **American Football Conference (AFC)**.

At the same time, another team would replace the old one in Cleveland. That team would be called the Browns and keep the club's history and records. The Ravens would be the NFL's "new" team—even though the roster was made up of players from Cleveland. Baltimore fans didn't care. They were just excited for the first season to begin.

Among the stars who switched uniforms were quarterback Vinny Testaverde and kicker Matt Stover. They were joined by a talented group of **rookie**s, including lineman Jonathan Ogden and linebacker Ray Lewis. The Ravens added more good players in the late 1990s, especially on defense. Jamie Sharper, Peter Boulware, Tony Siragusa, Rod Woodson, and Chris McAlister moved fast and tackled hard.

After three losing seasons, the Ravens finished 8–8 in 1999. One year later, they won 12 games and made the **playoffs** for the first time. The defense allowed only 165 points and gave up just 970 rushing yards.

The Baltimore offense came alive, too. Coach Brian Billick made a big difference. He was a genius when it came to the passing attack. Billick worked with quarterback Trent Dilfer and turned him into an excellent leader. Billick also gave rookie Jamal Lewis a chance. The powerful running back gained 1,364 yards. A key to his excellent season was the leadership shown by Priest Holmes.

LEFT: Vinny Testaverde fires a pass.
ABOVE: Jamal Lewis runs to the end zone.

7

Holmes had been the starter and a very productive player. He agreed to teach Lewis how to be a star in the NFL.

In the 2000 **postseason**, the Ravens *dominated* opponents with their defense. They won three playoff games and gave up a total of only 16 points. In **Super Bowl** XXXV, the Ravens continued their amazing roll by defeating the New York Giants, 34–7. In just three seasons, Baltimore had risen to the top of *professional* football and thrilled a new *generation* of fans with an NFL championship.

After their Super Bowl victory, the Ravens built on their *tradition* as a hard-hitting team. Lewis and McAlister formed the heart of the defense. They were joined by new stars Ed Reed and Terrell Suggs. Lewis and Reed were each

LEFT: Ray Lewis was the heart and soul of the Ravens for 16 seasons.
ABOVE: Ed Reed specialized in returning interceptions for touchdowns.

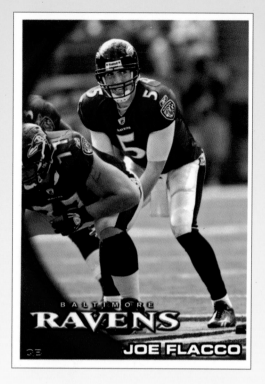

recognized for their great play as the NFL's Defensive Player of the Year.

The Ravens also had the makings of a good offense. Running back Willis McGahee, tight end Todd Heap, and receiver Derrick Mason all developed into excellent players. Baltimore fans hoped their team would return to the Super Bowl, but their great defense was not enough to win another title by itself. The Ravens needed a winning quarterback.

In 2008, Billick stepped aside, and John Harbaugh became the Baltimore coach. Harbaugh placed his faith in a rookie quarterback named Joe Flacco. It was a good decision. Flacco had a great arm and a *competitive* spirit. His confidence rubbed off on young running backs Ray Rice and Le'Ron McClain. Rice became one of the NFL's most dangerous weapons.

In 2008, the Ravens made it to the playoffs as a **Wild Card** and came within one victory of returning to the Super Bowl. In the years that followed, Baltimore continued to live up to its *reputation* as a great defensive team. New stars moved into the lineup, including Haloti Ngata, Dawan Landry, and Lardarius Webb. The team

finished atop the **AFC North** in 2010 and 2011 and gave the fans a lot to get excited about. The Ravens have shown that they know what it takes to win—a strong defense, timely offense, and lots of team spirit.

LEFT: This trading card shows Joe Flacco eyeing the defense.
ABOVE: Ray Rice cuts to his left on a running play.

Home Turf

The Ravens didn't have their own stadium during their first two seasons in Baltimore. They played in Memorial Stadium, which had once been the home of the Colts. In 1998, the team moved into a new stadium that was originally called Ravens Stadium at Camden Yards. It is right next to Oriole Park at Camden Yards, the home of the Orioles baseball team.

The Ravens' stadium had a grass field when it opened. In 2003, the team changed to *artificial turf.* The area in front of the stadium's main entrance is called Unitas Plaza, named in memory of Colts hero Johnny Unitas. Fans pass a bronze statue of the great quarterback as they walk toward the stadium.

BY THE NUMBERS

- The Ravens' stadium has 71,008 seats.
- The stadium cost $220 million to build.
- The stadium has two huge video screens. Each measures 24 feet high and 100 feet wide.

On game days in Baltimore, the Ravens' stadium is a sea of purple.

Dressed for Success

Baltimore's colors are purple, black, white, and metallic gold. The team's helmet is black with a purple raven's head that has the letter *B* on it. For some games, the Ravens wear an all-black uniform. It reminds some fans of a raven, which is all black, too.

The *inspiration* for Baltimore's name came from a poem called "The Raven" by Edgar Allan Poe. He was a famous writer who made Baltimore his home for many years. Poe was also a cousin of Maryland's Attorney General, John Prentiss Poe, whose sons were football stars more than a century ago.

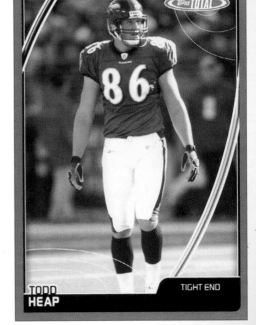

The Ravens have three *mascots*— Edgar, Allan, and Poe. The name of the team was chosen from suggestions that included Marauders and Americans. More than 30,000 fans voted in the naming contest.

LEFT: Haloti Ngata wears the Ravens' home colors.
RIGHT: As this Todd Heap trading card shows, Baltimore's uniform has changed little over the past decade.

We Won!

There's an old saying in sports that defense wins championships. The Ravens proved that to be true in 2000. Few teams in NFL history have been as dominant. During that season, Baltimore gave up just 165 points. That was the lowest total of any team since the NFL went to a 16-game schedule in the 1970s.

The Ravens had stars at every position on defense. Linemen Sam Adams and Tony Siragusa clogged up the middle on running plays. Linebacker Ray Lewis led a fearsome group of pass-rushers that included Peter Boulware, Rob Burnett, and Jamie Sharper. Rod Woodson, Chris McAlister, and Duane Starks were the heart of a talented **secondary**.

The Ravens went 12–4 during the regular season, including seven wins in a row in November and December. Their record was good

LEFT: Peter Boulware sizes up the competition.
RIGHT: The Baltimore defense smothered the Tennessee Titans during the 2000 playoffs.

enough for a Wild Card spot in the playoffs. Baltimore played the Denver Broncos in the first round of the postseason. The defense held the Broncos to 42 rushing yards and **sacked** quarterback Gus Frerotte five times. On offense, Jamal Lewis ran for 110 yards and two touchdowns. The Ravens won easily, 21–3.

Next up for Baltimore were the Tennessee Titans. The Ravens had finished behind them in the **AFC Central**. Both teams had great defenses. Everyone expected a close game.

The Titans took an early 7–0 lead, but the Baltimore defense soon took control. With the score tied 10–10 in the fourth quarter, the Ravens blocked a **field goal**, and Anthony Mitchell returned it 90 yards for a touchdown. A short time later, Ray Lewis **intercepted** a pass and ran it back 50 yards for a score. Baltimore celebrated a 24–10 victory.

The Ravens then faced the Oakland Raiders for the AFC championship. The defense got the job done again. Baltimore recorded four interceptions and four sacks, and Oakland gained just 24 yards on the ground. The offense made a big contribution in the second quarter when Trent Dilfer threw a short pass from his own end zone to Shannon Sharpe. The Baltimore tight end powered his way down the field for a 96-yard touchdown. It was the longest passing play in team history. That was all the offense that the Ravens needed. They won 16–3.

Two weeks later, Baltimore met the New York Giants in Super Bowl XXXV. The Ravens were very confident. They had not lost a game since the end of October. Their fans were eager for the team's first championship.

The Ravens again set the tone with their defense. Meanwhile, Dilfer threw a long touchdown pass to Brandon Stokely, and Matt Stover added a field goal for a 10–0 lead. In the third quarter, Starks intercepted a pass at midfield and ran it back for a touchdown. Moments later, Ron Dixon of the Giants returned the Baltimore kickoff for a touchdown. The score was now 17–7.

The Ravens quickly regrouped, thanks to Jermaine Lewis. He caught the next kickoff on his 16-yard line, weaved his way down the field, and went all the way for a touchdown. Baltimore moved ahead 24–7. The Ravens added 10 points in the fourth quarter for a 34–10 victory. Ray Lewis was named the game's **Most Valuable Player (MVP)**.

LEFT: The Oakland Raiders can't catch Shannon Sharpe on his 96-yard touchdown.　　**ABOVE**: Ray Lewis shows the fans who's number one!

Go-To Guys

To be a true star in the NFL, you need more than fast feet and a big body. You have to be a "go-to guy"—someone the coach wants on the field at the end of a big game. Ravens fans have had a lot to cheer about over the years, including these great stars …

THE PIONEERS

JONATHAN OGDEN — Offensive Lineman

- BORN: 7/31/1974   • PLAYED FOR TEAM: 1996 TO 2007

Jonathan Ogden was the first player ever **drafted** by the Ravens. Ogden stood 6′ 9″ and weighed 340 pounds, but he was also quick and *agile*. Many fans believe that he was the best left tackle in NFL history.

RAY LEWIS — Linebacker

- BORN: 5/15/1975   • FIRST YEAR WITH TEAM: 1996

Ray Lewis was the most feared and respected defensive player in the league. He could do it all—chase down running backs, sack the quarterback, and intercept passes. Lewis was named All-Pro seven times from 1999 to 2009.

TONY SIRAGUSA   Defensive Lineman

- BORN: 5/14/1967   • PLAYED FOR TEAM: 1997 TO 2001

Tony Siragusa powered through opponents like a bulldozer. He teamed with Sam Adams to give Baltimore a great defensive line. Fans and teammates also loved Siragusa for his sense of humor.

PETER BOULWARE   Linebacker

- BORN: 12/18/1974   • PLAYED FOR TEAM: 1997 TO 2005

Peter Boulware was Baltimore's first choice in the 1997 draft. He was at his best when rushing the quarterback. Boulware made the **Pro Bowl** four times and retired as the Ravens' all-time leader in sacks.

JAMIE SHARPER   Linebacker

- BORN: 11/23/1974   • PLAYED FOR TEAM: 1997 TO 2001

Jamie Sharper learned a lot playing alongside Ray Lewis. In his five seasons with the Ravens, he had 14 sacks, intercepted two passes, and recovered a **fumble** three times.

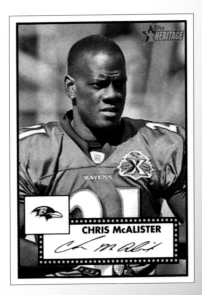

CHRIS McALISTER   Defensive Back

- BORN: 6/14/1977   • PLAYED FOR TEAM: 1999 TO 2008

Chris McAlister became a star for the Ravens when he intercepted five passes in his rookie season. He only got better after that. McAlister was named **All-Pro** in 2003 and made the Pro Bowl three times.

LEFT: Jonathan Ogden
RIGHT: Chris McAlister

JAMAL LEWIS   Running Back

• BORN: 8/26/1979   • PLAYED FOR TEAM: 2000 TO 2006

When Jamal Lewis joined the Ravens, he transformed the team's rushing attack. Lewis was a fast and powerful runner who never seemed to get tired. In 2000, he became just the fifth player in history to gain 2,000 yards in a season.

TODD HEAP   Tight End

• BORN: 3/16/1980   • PLAYED FOR TEAM: 2001 TO 2010

For many years, Todd Heap was the secret weapon in Baltimore's passing game. He could always find a soft spot in the defense. In 2003, Heap led the Ravens in receptions and made the Pro Bowl.

ED REED   Defensive Back

• BORN: 9/11/1978   • FIRST YEAR WITH TEAM: 2002

Ed Reed was a star from the first day he stepped on the field for the Ravens. In 2004, Reed led the NFL in interceptions and was named Defensive Player of the Year. Over his first 10 seasons, he scored eight touchdowns.

TERRELL SUGGS   Linebacker/Defensive Lineman

• BORN: 10/11/1982   • FIRST YEAR WITH TEAM: 2003

Terrell Suggs loved to rush the quarterback. In his rookie season, he had 12 sacks. Eight years later, Suggs had the best season of his career and was named the 2011 NFL Defensive Player of the Year.

HALOTI NGATA Defensive Lineman

- BORN: 1/21/1984 • FIRST YEAR WITH TEAM: 2006

The Ravens had never used their first pick in the draft on a defensive lineman until Haloti Ngata came along. They made a good decision. Ngata was a great all-around athlete. He was voted All-Pro in 2010 and 2011.

RAY RICE Running Back

- BORN: 1/22/1987 • FIRST YEAR WITH TEAM: 2008

Ray Rice was equally dangerous as a runner and a receiver. Though he stood just 5′ 9″ and weighed less than 200 pounds, he was very *durable*. In 2011, Rice gained more than 2,000 yards, and only one other player in the NFL touched the ball more often than he did.

JOE FLACCO Quarterback

- BORN: 1/16/1985
- FIRST YEAR WITH TEAM: 2008

Joe Flacco didn't go to a powerhouse college, so some experts questioned whether he could be successful in the NFL. Flacco proved them wrong. He led the Ravens to the playoffs in each of his first four seasons and threw 80 touchdown passes during that period.

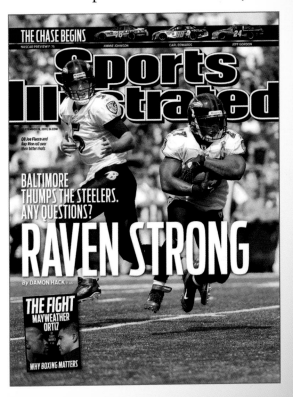

RIGHT: Ray Rice takes a handoff from Joe Flacco on the cover of *Sports Illustrated*.

Calling the Shots

Hiring a head coach in the NFL is never an easy decision. For the Ravens in 1996, that choice was more complicated than usual. They needed a coach that Baltimore fans knew. They also wanted someone who was familiar with the players coming over from Cleveland. The solution was to hire Ted Marchibroda.

Marchibroda had coached the Colts in the 1970s when they played in Baltimore. He liked the city, and the fans liked him. One of his first moves was to add Ozzie Newsome as an assistant coach. Newsome had been a star for the Browns in the 1970s and 1980s. The pair worked together to build Baltimore into a winner. Later, Newsome became the first African-American *general manager* in NFL history.

In 1999, Brian Billick was brought in to coach the Ravens. He had previously turned the Minnesota Vikings into an offensive powerhouse. Billick focused on doing the same in Baltimore. He added skilled offensive players, and the Ravens quickly became one of the top teams in the NFL. In 2000, he led them to their first championship.

Brian Billick raises the Super Bowl trophy.

In 2008, John Harbaugh was named coach of the Ravens. He came from a great football family. His brother, Jim, had played quarterback in the NFL and later became the coach of the San Francisco 49ers. Harbaugh was *intense* and organized. Nothing ever slipped by him. The Ravens played in the **AFC Championship Game** in two of his first four seasons.

One Great Day

The Ravens will always have a special link to the Cleveland Browns. That makes every game between the two teams a little more exciting. The Ravens and Browns met for the first time on the field in 2003. Before the game, Jamal Lewis phoned his friend Andra Davis, a linebacker for the Browns. The pair laughed when Lewis predicted that he would break the NFL record for rushing yards in a game. It turned out that he wasn't joking.

On Baltimore's second play of the game, Lewis took a handoff and raced through the Cleveland defense for an 82-yard touchdown. By halftime, the Ravens had the lead, and Lewis had pushed his rushing total to 180 yards. As Lewis walked into the locker room, offensive lineman Jonathan Ogden said to him, "We can get 300 yards."

Lewis took those words to heart. With the Ravens up by a field goal at the beginning of the fourth quarter, Lewis made another long run. This time, he went 63 yards for a touchdown.

The Browns can only watch as Jamal Lewis streaks toward the end zone.

Baltimore ended up winning 33–13, but the real excitement surrounded Lewis. Would he break the record of 278 yards in a game? With just under seven minutes left, Lewis did it. But he wasn't done. Lewis finished with 295 yards!

After the game, someone pointed out that Lewis might have finished with more than 350 yards. In the second quarter, a 60-yard run had been wiped out because of a teammate's penalty. "On a day like today, I can't regret anything," Lewis said. "It was beautiful."

Legend Has It

Who was the nicest Raven?

LEGEND HAS IT that Jonathan Ogden was. Playing in the NFL is serious business. The sport is rough, and winning is the most important goal. Players usually put on their "game face" before kickoff. Ogden was different. He was always smiling. "He's a laugher," All-Pro defender Michael Strahan once said. "You think to yourself, this guy is not mean enough to handle the mean guys out there in the NFL." Of course, Ogden was. He made the Pro Bowl 11 times and was voted All-Pro nine times.

ABOVE: Jonathan Ogden is shown in a rare serious moment.

Which quarterback had the most impressive start in NFL history?

LEGEND HAS IT that Joe Flacco did. In 2008, he led the Ravens to the playoffs as a rookie—and then won two postseason games. In the years that followed, Flacco only got better. In 2009, 2010, and 2011, he guided the Ravens back to the playoffs and produced at least one postseason victory each year. No one in NFL history had ever done that before.

Which Baltimore defender did opponents try to avoid at all costs?

LEGEND HAS IT that it was Ed Reed. Not only was Reed good at breaking up passes, he was great at intercepting them—and then running them back for touchdowns. Even so, some quarterbacks could not resist trying to throw the ball Reed's way. In the first game of the 2011 season, Reed had two interceptions against the Pittsburgh Steelers. It was the 12th time he had picked off more than one pass in the same game, which set an NFL record.

For John Harbaugh and his brother, Jim, coaching is a family affair. John was hired to lead the Ravens in 2008. Three years later, Jim became the coach of the San Francisco 49ers. One of the first calls he got was from John. The two had a lot to talk about. The Ravens were scheduled to host the 49ers in late November.

This would be a historic day. Brothers had never coached against each other in the NFL. As the game neared, fans in San Francisco and Baltimore got more and more excited. What made things especially interesting was that both teams were playing well. The Ravens had won seven of their first 10 games and were in first place in the AFC North. The 49ers had an even better record at 9–1.

The Ravens got bad news before the game. Ray Lewis, the leader of the Baltimore defense, was hurt and could not play. That put pressure on the rest of the Ravens. They would have to pick up the slack without Lewis on the field.

To no one's surprise, the game was a tense struggle from the opening kickoff. The Ravens tied a team record with nine sacks. They also recovered a fumble. The score was tied 6–6 in the fourth quarter

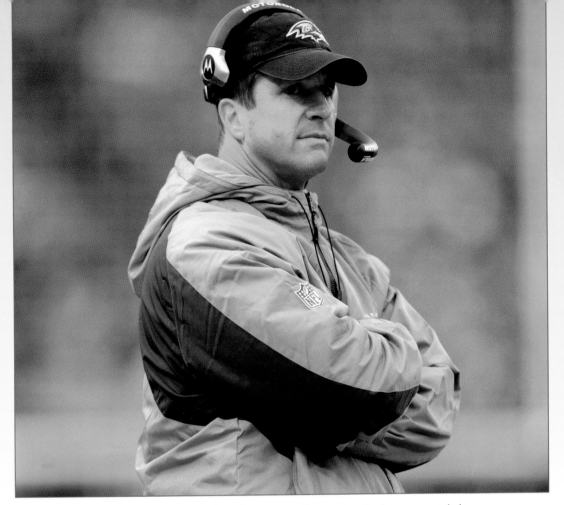

John Harbaugh watches his team from the Baltimore sidelines.

when Joe Flacco fired a touchdown pass to tight end Dennis Pitta. The Ravens took a 13–6 lead.

San Francisco tried to fight back, but the Baltimore defense was too tough. The Ravens went on to win, 16–6. When John and Jim met at midfield after the game, they gave each other a long hug. Up in the stands, two proud parents—Jack and Jackie Harbaugh—stood and cheered.

Team Spirit

Baltimore football fans are unmatched in the NFL. Their lives revolve around the Ravens. When the team wins, they have an extra bounce in their step. When the Ravens lose, they hurt inside. This tradition goes back to the days when the Colts played in Baltimore.

How much do Baltimore fans love football? After the Colts left town in 1984, the fans adopted a team in Canada and gathered in big crowds to watch them play. This caught the attention of Art Modell, who was looking for a new home for the Cleveland Browns. He was impressed enough to choose Baltimore.

The Ravens understand the importance of their connection to their fans. The team encourages the players to give back to the community in all sorts of ways. Since their first season, the Ravens have raised millions of dollars for the sick and needy.

LEFT: Hey you! Baltimore fans aren't afraid to scream at opposing players—or their own players!
ABOVE: This pin celebrates the team's Super Bowl victory.

n this timeline, each Super Bowl is listed under the year it was played. Remember that the Super Bowl is held early in the year and is actually part of the previous season. For example, Super Bowl XLVI was played on February 5, 2012, but it was the championship of the 2011 NFL season.

1998
Priest Holmes rushes for more than 1,000 yards.

2002
Jonathan Ogden is named All-Pro for the third time.

1996
The Ravens play their first season.

2000
Ray Lewis is named Defensive Player of the Year.

2001
The Ravens win Super Bowl XXXV.

Jermaine Lewis celebrates a touchdown during Baltimore's Super Bowl win.

Mark Clayton led the 2006 team with 939 receiving yards.

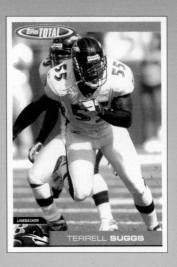

Terrell Suggs

2006
The Ravens go 13–3 in the regular season.

2008
John Harbaugh becomes the coach.

2011
Terrell Suggs leads the team with 14 sacks.

2004
Ed Reed is named Defensive Player of the Year.

2009
Ray Rice and Le'Ron McClain make the Pro Bowl.

2010
Kicker Billy Cundiff is named All-Pro.

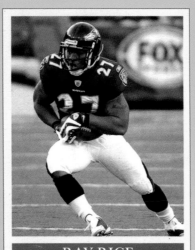

Ray Rice

Fun Facts

FIRST IMPRESSIONS

On opening day of the 2008 season, the Ravens beat the Cincinnati Bengals, 17–10. It was the first time in history a rookie quarterback (Joe Flacco) and rookie coach (John Harbaugh) both won in their NFL *debut*.

FOUR SCORE

In 2003, Marcus Robinson set the team record for touchdown catches in a game. In an exciting 44–41 victory over the Seattle Seahawks, he scored four times—all in the second half!

RICE IS NICE

Few runners have ever been as fast in the open field as Ray Rice. In a 2010 playoff game against the New England Patriots, Rice ran 83 yards for a touchdown on Baltimore's first play. It was the second-longest run in NFL postseason history.

ABOVE: Marcus Robinson catches a touchdown pass against the Seattle Seahawks.   **RIGHT**: Ed Reed heads for the end zone after intercepting a pass.

BREAKING GOOD

In 2004, Ed Reed set an NFL record when he intercepted a pass in his own end zone and ran it back 106 yards for a touchdown. That mark lasted until 2008, when Reed returned an interception 107 yards to break his own record.

PICK ME UP

When Ray Lewis missed 11 games in 2002, fans wondered who would fill in for him. The answer was Ed Hartwell. He made 142 tackles that season!

ISLAND LIFE

Ma'ake Kemoeatu played for the Ravens from 2002 to 2005. He was one of many NFL players to star for Kahuku High School in Hawaii.

Talking Football

"A nickname for our defense? How about *The Best*."
▶ **Tony Siragusa,** *on the 2000 Ravens*

"You pay attention to detail, you do the best job you can, and good things happen."
▶ **John Harbaugh,** *on what it takes to become a successful coach in the NFL*

"A lot of times that is what keeps us **motivated** to never stop, even when the times get tough."
▶ **Ray Lewis,** *on the love and support of Baltimore fans*

"Each game can be won in different ways. I've tried to **hone** that skill as much as others have honed throwing."

► *Trent Dilfer, on the secret of being a winner*

"He's never rattled. He's always got that look on his face like he's calm."

► *Todd Heap, on why Joe Flacco's nickname was "Joe Cool"*

"I am responsible for everything that goes on with this football team. The buck stops here."

► *Brian Billick, on the pressure of being an NFL coach*

"When I'm running, I'm looking for contact. It's kind of weird. It brings a fire to me."

► *Ray Rice, on why he doesn't run away from tacklers*

LEFT: Tony Siragusa   **ABOVE**: Trent Dilfer

Great Debates

People who root for the Ravens love to compare their favorite moments, teams, and players. Some debates have been going on for years! How would you settle these classic football arguments?

Ray Lewis was the Ravens' greatest defensive star ....

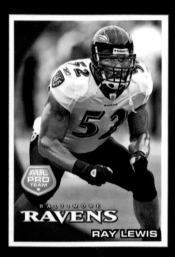

… because the record says so. Lewis (**LEFT**) was an All-Pro seven times from 1999 to 2009. He was also picked for 13 Pro Bowls and earned recognition as Defensive Player of the Year twice. To top it off, Lewis was the MVP of Super Bowl XXXV. Lewis led the Ravens in tackles 12 times and was also an excellent pass defender. Simply put, he was the best.

Not so fast. Ed Reed was the better player ....

… because he was Baltimore's last line of defense. If Lewis missed a tackle or made a mistake, Reed was always there to save the day. Despite this incredible pressure, Reed dared quarterbacks and receivers to challenge him. The result was more than 50 interceptions. Heading into 2012, Reed had returned eight for touchdowns.

Todd Heap was Baltimore's best tight end ....

… because the Ravens could always count on him to do his job. On most plays, he was a key blocker in the running game. But when the Ravens needed a first down, Heap (RIGHT) was often the target of choice. He caught more than 50 passes five times from 2002 to 2009 and scored 41 touchdowns during his Baltimore career.

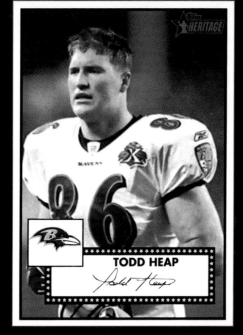

TODD HEAP

There's no argument here. Shannon Sharpe wins hands down ....

… because without him, the Ravens may not have won Super Bowl XXXV. Sharpe played only two seasons for Baltimore, but he was the team's most dangerous weapon, with 140 catches. His 96-yard touchdown catch against the Oakland Raiders in the AFC Championship Game gave the Ravens the points they needed to reach the Super Bowl.

For the Record

The great Ravens teams and players have left their marks on the record books. These are the "best of the best" …

RAVENS AWARD WINNERS

WINNER	AWARD	YEAR
Peter Boulware	Defensive Rookie of the Year	1997
Ray Lewis	Defensive Player of the Year	2000
Ray Lewis	Super Bowl XXXV MVP	2000
Terrell Suggs	Defensive Rookie of the Year	2003
Jamal Lewis	Offensive Player of the Year	2003
Ray Lewis	Defensive Player of the Year	2003
Ed Reed	Defensive Player of the Year	2004

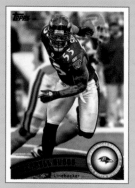

Terrell Suggs

Ed Reed

Ray Lewis

RAVENS ACHIEVEMENTS

ACHIEVEMENT	YEAR
Super Bowl XXXV Champions	2000*
AFC North Champions	2003
AFC North Champions	2006
AFC North Champions	2010
AFC North Champions	2011

Super Bowls are played early the following year, but the game is counted as the championship of this season.

ABOVE: Chris McAlister intercepted a pass in Super Bowl XXXV.
LEFT: Rob Burnett celebrates a Super Bowl sack on the cover of *The Sporting News*.

Pinpoints

The history of a football team is made up of many smaller stories. These stories take place all over the map—not just in the city a team calls "home." Match the pushpins on these maps to the **Team Facts**, and you will begin to see the story of the Ravens unfold!

TEAM FACTS

1 Baltimore, Maryland—*The team has played here since 1996.*

2 Brooklyn, New York—*Vinny Testaverde was born here.*

3 Detroit, Michigan—*Derrick Mason was born here.*

4 Columbia, South Carolina—*Peter Boulware was born here.*

5 Fort Wayne, Indiana—*Rod Woodson was born here.*

6 Chicago, Illinois—*Shannon Sharpe was born here.*

7 Fort Smith, Arkansas—*Priest Holmes was born here.*

8 Minneapolis, Minnesota—*Terrell Suggs was born here.*

9 St. Rose, Louisiana—*Ed Reed was born here.*

10 Tampa, Florida—*The Ravens won Super Bowl XXXV here.*

11 Valley Center, California—*Billy Cundiff was born here.*

12 Tonga—*Ma'ake Kemoeatu was born here.*

Priest Holmes

12

Glossary

Football Words
Vocabulary Words

AFC CENTRAL—A division for teams that play in the central part of the country.

AFC CHAMPIONSHIP GAME—The game played to determine which AFC team will go to the Super Bowl.

AFC NORTH—A division for teams that play in the northern part of the country.

AGILE—Quick and graceful.

ALL-PRO—An honor given to the best players at their positions at the end of each season.

AMERICAN FOOTBALL CONFERENCE (AFC)—One of two groups of teams that make up the NFL.

ARTIFICIAL TURF—A playing surface made from fake grass.

COMPETITIVE—Having a strong desire to win.

DEBUT—First appearance.

DOMINATED—Controlled completely with the use of force.

DRAFTED—Chosen from a group of the best college players. The NFL draft is held each spring.

DURABLE—Able to avoid or withstand injury.

FIELD GOAL—A goal from the field, kicked over the crossbar and between the goal posts. A field goal is worth three points.

FUMBLE—A ball that is dropped by the player carrying it.

GENERAL MANAGER—A person who oversees all parts of a company.

GENERATION—A period of years roughly equal to the time it takes for a person to be born, grow up, and have children.

HONE—Sharpen or improve.

INSPIRATION—Someone or something that motivates others.

INTENSE—Extremely serious.

INTERCEPTED—Caught in the air by a defensive player.

MASCOTS—Animals or people believed to bring a group good luck.

MOST VALUABLE PLAYER (MVP)—The award given each year to the league's best player; also given to the best player in the Super Bowl and Pro Bowl.

MOTIVATED—Inspired to achieve.

NATIONAL FOOTBALL LEAGUE (NFL)—The league that started in 1920 and is still operating today.

PLAYOFFS—The games played after the regular season to determine which teams play in the Super Bowl.

POSTSEASON—Another term for playoffs.

PRO BOWL—The NFL's all-star game, played after the regular season.

PROFESSIONAL—Paid to play.

REPUTATION—A belief or opinion about someone or something.

ROOKIE—A player in his first year.

SACKED—Tackled the quarterback behind the line of scrimmage.

SECONDARY—The part of the defense made up by the cornerbacks and safeties.

SUPER BOWL—The championship of the NFL, played between the winners of the National Football Conference and AFC.

TRADITION—A belief or custom that is handed down from generation to generation.

WILD CARD—A team that makes the playoffs without winning its division.

OVERTIME

TEAM SPIRIT introduces a great way to stay up to date with your team! Visit our **OVERTIME** link and get connected to the latest and greatest updates. **OVERTIME** serves as a young reader's ticket to an exclusive web page—with more stories, fun facts, team records, and photos of the Ravens. Content is updated during and after each season. The **OVERTIME** feature also enables readers to send comments and letters to the author! Log onto:

www.norwoodhousepress.com/library.aspx

and click on the tab: **TEAM SPIRIT** to access **OVERTIME**.

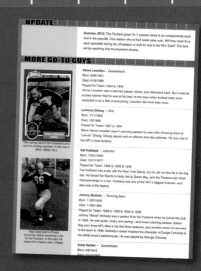

Read all the books in the series to learn more about professional sports. For a complete listing of the baseball, basketball, football, and hockey teams in the **TEAM SPIRIT** series, visit our website at:

www.norwoodhousepress.com/library.aspx

On the Road

BALTIMORE RAVENS
1101 Russell Street
Baltimore, Maryland 21230
410-261-7283
www.baltimoreravens.com

THE PRO FOOTBALL HALL OF FAME
2121 George Halas Drive NW
Canton, Ohio 44708
330-456-8207
www.profootballhof.com

On the Bookshelf

To learn more about the sport of football, look for these books at your library or bookstore:

- Frederick, Shane. *The Best of Everything Football Book.* North Mankato, Minnesota: Capstone Press, 2011.

- Jacobs, Greg. *The Everything Kids' Football Book: The All-Time Greats, Legendary Teams, Today's Superstars—And Tips on Playing Like a Pro.* Avon, Massachusetts: Adams Media Corporation, 2010.

- Editors of *Sports Illustrated for Kids. 1st and 10: Top 10 Lists of Everything in Football.* New York, New York: Sports Illustrated Books, 2011.

Index

About the Author

MARK STEWART has written more than 50 books on football and over 150 sports books for kids. He grew up in New York City during the 1960s rooting for the Giants and Jets, and was lucky enough to meet players from both teams. Mark comes from a family of writers. His grandfather was Sunday Editor of *The New York Times,* and his mother was Articles Editor of *Ladies' Home Journal* and *McCall's.* Mark has profiled hundreds of athletes over the past 25 years. He has also written several books about his native New York and New Jersey, his home today. Mark is a graduate of Duke University, with a degree in history. He lives and works in a home overlooking Sandy Hook, New Jersey. You can contact Mark through the Norwood House Press website.